C000215843

JACK & BILL
AND THE
FOGRUNT AMULET

A Poem
Volume 1
The Brothers Grime

Illustrations and map by CC and JH

IRON
PRESS

First published 2019 by IRON Press
5 Marden Terrace
Cullercoats
North Shields
NE30 4PD
tel +44(0)191 2531901
ironpress@xlnmail.com
www.ironpress.co.uk

ISBN 978-0-9954579-7-3
Printed by Imprint Digital

© The poems The Brothers Grime 2019
© Artwork CC & JH 2019
© This book, IRON Press 2019

Cover and book design Brian Grogan and Peter Mortimer

Typeset in Georgia 9pt
Image Photography by Kirstie Mackin

IRON Press books are distributed by
NBN International
and represented by Inpress Ltd
Churchill House, 12 Mosley Street,
Newcastle upon Tyne, NE1 1DE
tel: +44(0)191 2308104
www.inpressbooks.co.uk

Supported using public funding by
ARTS COUNCIL ENGLAND
LOTTERY FUNDED

The Brothers Grime

The Brothers Grime met in the late 1970s at school in High Wycombe. They began writing Jack and Bill poems in maths lessons, swapping verses under their desks. They were never caught and are still at it forty years on. They still know nothing of logarithms, equations or any of that old toss.

Your Guide
Through Cloudland

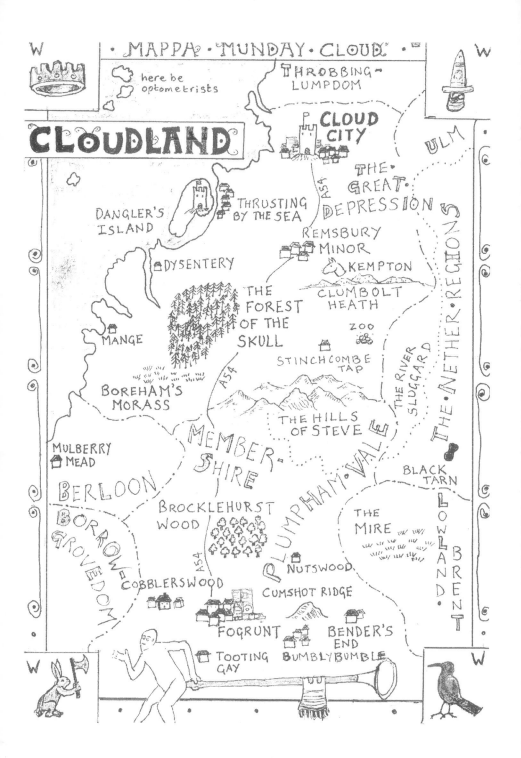

Historical Background

THIS EXTRACT, TAKEN FROM THE WORKS OF CLOUDLAND'S GREATEST historian, Bernie of Black Tarn, was both seed and sustenance to our enterprise. Given here in the original Middle Cloudish, it details the events that foreshadow our poem and sets the scene for our heroes' struggle.

And lo! Just as boil bulgeth youthen brow, so did sun push yellow head above horizon. And in the light of that pustule all Cloudland was at peace. Sea mists did ebb and flow from the cave-nostrilled cliffs like skeins of happy phlegm. Gulls unfurled the banners of their wings and kwarked their joy.

 And lo! The source of that peace did sit at village Mulberry Mead. Long time Mother Feakle did smile, knit and make jewellery from her gold-white hair. And all was balm and sloe cake until turd-shod tramp came knocking. For Mother Feakle did run as this demon of the verge did take out his thigh maggot, coax it and spread his seed upon her garden. And then he did steal her most precious makeling, The Fogrunt Amulet, in whose golden clasp lay Cloudland's fate. Then did grow from that loin of earth a purple-headed flower clept The Magic Donger.

 And lo! Slit-mouthed bloom spake filth unto all and dampen overcoat of gloom did lie o'er the land. Mother Feakle was fled to the timber-fingered Forest of the Skull and change-ed into bristle-stone beast, The Forty-Teated Sow.

 And yea! 'Twas wrote on scrapen walls that a witch queen would reign, only to be o'erthrown when sow and amulet are met at castle of the King, and that only by the hands of heroes famed as Jack and Bill would peace arise and Donger fall.

(From The Dog-Skin Histories of Cloudland)

This, the first volume of our narrative, consists of four books and takes us from its beginning to round about its middle. The second volume is forthcoming, but for reasons to do with length, girth and decency cannot be got out and placed in your hands just yet. Publication by instalment was how they used to do it in the old days and, as everybody knows, the old days were the best. Gentle readers, come join us then in Cloudland, and learn of how evil was once triumphed over by low-level depravity. Away! Let's away!

The Brothers Grime

1

Dramatis Personae:

Jack
a strapping lad

Bill
a giant

King Wobblyknobble
ruler of all Cloudland

Kitty Flaps
sullen teenager chosen by destiny

Wizard Dave
wizard to the court of King Wobblyknobble

Gossamergonk
fairy disguised as the brown moth Blue

Mr Flaps
father of Kitty

Mrs Dotty Flaps
wife of Mr Flaps, mother to Kitty

Nan Flaps
grandmother of Kitty and wrestling fan

The Forty-Teated Sow
the sleeping Mother Feakle, Kitty's true parent

Fleabag Barry
apothecary of Fogrunt town

Richard
kipper stall assistant and key to Cloudland's fate

Bernard Smethurst
leader of Cobblerswood Parish Council

Mrs Smethurst
Overmaiden of The Feakle Maidens of Berloon

Reverend Godfrey Scrimp
vicar of Cobblerswood

Jim Rix
neighbour of the Flaps family, lecher

Leslie 'Fat Boy' Jeavons
Fogrunt bus driver

Cheeky Pete
lepidopterist to the royal court

Old Dick
King Wobblyknobble's personal barber

Dwayne 'Jive Man' Malone
Cloudland's top pop-singing heartthrob

Granny D-Cup
Cloudland's favourite old-aged pin-up

Reg Swizell
zoo keeper

Donny Stoat
stoat

Book One: Such Gossip Amongst the Rooks

Part One:

*Our heroes Jack and Bill are charged with
a mission for the King of Cloudland*

Cobblerswood

A bustling throng in Cobblerswood
Had gathered for this special day;
They'd come, the old, the young, the good,
To see him as he passed this way –
They stood outside their little houses,
Chaps in shirts, 'for best' smart trousers,
Ladies wore their brightest blouses,
All was grand. "Hip! Hip! Hooray!"

"Long live the King!" a small girl cried,
"Long may he reign!" the crowd replied;
"Over us all," a fat man said,
"Yes," they agreed, nodding their heads.

Even three pickpockets stopped to cheer
As the golden coach comes rumbling near;
They waved a wallet, watch and truss,
"King Wobblyknobble's one of us!"

The king was on his annual tour
Around the Cloudland nation,
To reap his tax of coin and grain,
And love and adulation.

His fawning subjects thought him great,
A glance made worthwhile three hours' wait,
He gave a condescending smile,
Waved a damp hand a little while,
Flicked bogeys at the upturned faces;
Sordid, yet with airs and graces.

Some village folk on hands and knees
Collect these lumps of dried-up sneeze,
For baubles from the royal snout
Are prized as heirlooms hereabouts.

A shabby voice from up above
Urged "Quick! Stoop down and get one, love!"
The oik swayed on his shouldery perch,
Unbalanced as the giant lurched,
Pushed down a lady with a hat on –
"Sorry, Miss, I'm having that 'un!"

Too late those giant fingers reach,
A milkman nabs the snot;
The fallen jockey kicks his steed,
"Oh, Bill, you ten-foot clot!"

He showers ineffectual blows
Upon the bending ogre's nose;
"I wanted *that one* for myself
To show off on the dresser shelf!"

With unkempt air and bulbous nose,
Insolent glare, eleven toes,
Of meagre height, a sullen git,
Young Jack gets by on his half-wits.

The giant's older, with a paunch,
But loyal, steadfast, stupid, staunch;
Receding hair, with several chins,
A beard for keeping breakfast in;
Deep-set eyes, with heavy features,
Breath disgusting, like a teacher's.

The royal coach it floats away
Along the crowd-lined road;
An ingot passing down a sewer,
It bears its precious load.

Jack

Jack remounts the giant's shoulders,
Grabs the reins of that coarse beard:
"Let's go and do a bit of dogging–
Cleaning ladies, nothing weird."

They turn to meet the pressing swarm
That's heading from the village square;
Get quite caught up, carried along,
Then hear a voice call "Hoy! You there!"

A hawkish eye,
A wolfish grin,
A cracked and warty toadish skin,
A cloak as dark as wing of raven,
Cried Jack "It's Wizard Dave!"

And so it was, this bestial potion,
Stewing 'neath a pointy hat,
Was Wizard to the Court of Cloudland,
Bearded like a widow's twat.

"Psst!" called the wizard. "Quickly, lads!"
He beckoned to a darkened corner,
Gestured to a stuffed full bag –
"What is it now?" asked Jack the moaner.
"How'd yer like some dirty mags?
These'll satisfy yer boner!"

He rolled the top of the bag down,
Bit by bit,
Bit by bit.
Like an oily foreskin back it went,
Revealing just a hint of tit.
Jack jumped for joy: "My favourite mag!
Brawny Bird or Man in Drag?"

His hand slipped in and touched it but
The wizard slammed the opening shut.
"Before you get this treasured smut
I've got a little job for you;
It's quite straightforward, as you'll see,
A little... *erm*... delivery;
It's just some old... *erm*... jewellery –
A simple thing to do!"

"I must away with good King Wob,
For Court Wizard's a full-time job.
Get yourself to Fogrunt town,
Go past the stocks, *The Nose and Crown*,
And deep into the Wise Man Quarter,
Through that square where goats are slaughtered;
Turn at the gents lavs, please don't tarry,
Quick to the shop of Fleabag Barry."

Giant Bill

"I want you to collect a thing
Of highest value to the king;
A glittering trinket that was made
Long ago by the Feakle Maid –
A bracelet wrought from her gold hair,
That back in time was stole from her."

Jack huffs and puffs and shifts his feet,
But all the while his trouser meat
Distracts with thoughts of other stuff
"We'll do it, Dave, that's fair enough."

He makes to grab the wizard's stash,
So keen to give his tool a bash,
But Dave says "Boys, I'll want them back,
And don't go cutting out the cracks."

Who could have guessed? Who could have known?
Jack's thought of spending time alone –
Himself, these mags, his throbbing bone –
Would lead to so much trouble?
And consequences for the throne
Of Wobblyknobble?

Part Two

An unwitting threat sits waiting

No cosmic sign had warned the world,
No changeling had appeared;
No empire crumbled, scroll unfurled,
No evil sorcerer cheered;
No lightning flash, no thunderclaps,
No kingdom torn by bloody slaughter;
The day that Mrs Dotty Flaps
First set eyes on her titless daughter.

She'd passed, unnoticed, like a mouse,
With her mum and dad in their little house.

Yet sat, framed in a poster
For Thrusting-by-the-Sea,
("I hate that place, I hate that place,
It brings back memories,")
How could the girl have guessed she was
A lock without a key?

A chosen one, an eldritch,
Worse than any hag or harpy,
Termagant or witch;
Hex or banshee, evil crone,
Or gonk-collecting bitch.

Part Three

At Fogrunt Bus Station, momentous connections are almost made

By the gingham cloth of longitude and latitude
Fogrunt is a stain to Cloudland's south;
Stubborn and involuntary in attitude,
A drop of grease from its creator's mouth.

Translated from the near-forgotten early Cloudish tongue,
Fogrunt's ancient civic motto proudly stands
At every exit from the city, carved on monumental stones
Now kindly don't forget to wash your hands.

If Fogrunt's lanes are arteries,
Its black canal its lungs;
Mephitic parks its cancer cells,
Its folk a wagging tongue;
Then this must be its evil brain –
The place where buses run.

The pointless people huddled there,
The sense of tacky, grim despair;
Shoppers grasping plastic bags,
Listless school kids, strange men, hags
Returning to their shabby hovels,
Exhaust fumes choke the stinking air.

A listless school kid

Were we to seize those shopping bags
And spill their secret contents on the ground,
Would we find the broken fragments
Of some kind of once-shared dream
Being borne away and buried underground?
Underground?
Buried
In the heedless
Icy ground?

There she sits alone, Kitty Flaps;
Making her way home, Kitty Flaps;
While others sit around and chat
About *fucking this* and *sodding that*
No one's got much time for Kitty Flaps.

Her thoughts her own, ne'er spoke nor heard,
No friend she can confide in;
And, like a big bus terminal,
The world's a place to hide in.

Sixteen and slight,
And not very bright,
With breasts flat as pancakes
Her life seems a hard place –
Poor Kitty Flaps,
Kitty Flaps,
Kitty Flaps.

She watched the town vacate its bowels
As each bus pulled away;
Some goblins left for Scrote Estate,
A troll for Tooting Gay.

Some single mums with re-filled tums,
They made their way to seats
Which carried still fresh carvings
From the days when their young teats
Were being mauled by school boys
With names like *Baz* and *Zane*;
Instead of nose-pierced babies
Called *Dak* and *Britney—Jane*.

Kitty Flaps

A specky boy sat reading a book –
Kitty gave him a sideways look;
"He seems exciting," the poor girl thought,
Clutching the single she'd just bought –
Please Notice Me by Dwayne Malone
(She'd dance to it when she got home,
Her bedroom door shut, on her own);
The boy got the bus for Bender's End –
Her love affair was at an end.

"He never even saw me," thought Kitty.

Nor did two bent figures
Hurrying through the throng;
"Keep tight hold of your shopping, Bill,
Rather than your dong."

They'd spent a busy afternoon
In *The Orifice* shopping mall;
Buying those necessities
Without which life would pall.

Some cleansing powder for false teeth,
Some crotchless pants, a funeral wreath;
A rubber vagina, *just like the real thing*,
A bag of buns and a ball of string;
Some phallus-shaped shakers for salt and pepper,
Action transfers depicting a colony of lepers.

"There's one last chore we have to do,
For Wizard Dave, remember, who
Asked us to go and get that thing
Of such importance to the king;
It's with the old apothecary,
Fleabag Barry."

Fleabag dwelt down Earwax Lane
In Fogrunt's Wise Man Quarter;
They passed three fortune-tellers' shops,
A burnt-out tattoo parlour;
"It's one of the nicer parts of town,"
Said Jack, "If you don't mind squalor."

Part Four

At the house of the Apothecary, Jack and Bill collect a fateful item

At length they entered Fleabag's den,
But not a soul there could they spy;
Till, from a parlour door nearby,
They heard a low, impatient cry
Of long built-up frustration.

Bill, he gazed around the shop,
Like many a Saturday boy, took stock:
A human skull, a jar of ears;
A phial of naughty children's tears;
A demi-john of half-chewed dicks,
A box of nacks without their nicks;
A library on racing form;
A tin of stupid people's gorm;
A hundred pots of spells and ointments
Dignified *by Royal Appointment*.

He held a dusty crystal ball
With a broken horizontal hold;
A single image flickered there,
A single thing foretold.

He saw a faint but female form
Run, as through a dream;
A caption said *Bet Empress Dread
At Kempton, 3:15*.

Jack gave a knock at the parlour door
Then stopped and peered inside;
"I'll be with you in a minute, mate!"
The apothecary cried.
"Just hold on, I'll not keep you waiting –
I'll soon be finished masturbating."

A floorboard creaks,
A wheeze, a sigh,
A throaty cry of "Phwoar!"
The furtive sounds of self-abuse
Rebounded round the store.

A grunt, a groan,
A plop, a plink;
A teaspoon
Knocked into the sink.

Heavy breathing, muffled words:
"I love you more than all those birds!"
Jack gave a gasp, Fleabag was bent
Before a map of Lowland Brent.

Said Jack: "Hoy, can't you hurry up!
We've got a bus to get!"
And after five more minutes
He sighed "Ain't you finished yet?"
The apothecary, his task now botched,
Whined "It's difficult when you're being watched!"

Fleabag Barry

"Quick, Bill!" called Jack, "Get over here!
We've got to help this chap!
The only sort of curves he craves
Are contours on a map!
He'd swap the best pornography
For musty old cartography!"

A flash of Cloudland's favourite pin-up
Granny D-Cup did the trick.
Jack seldom ever left the house
Without his treasured, well-worn pic.

Fleabag buttoned up his fly,
A knowing twinkle in his eye:
"How can I help you out then, boys?
Some ointment for the haemorrhoids?"

Jack looked about him, dropped his voice,
Dropped his voice to a breath;
Dropped his voice as if Death
Itself was listening keenly in.

"We've come on a quest for Wizard Dave,
Be cautious, careful, please!"
But Bill, impatient, butted in:
"The Fogrunt Amulet, please!"

"Hush! Hush!" warned Fleabag,
"Stay your tongue!
Of this you must not speak!
For all around are watching eyes
Intent to gain this sacred prize!
But yes, I've got it, and it's mended;
I've straightened it where it was bended
When Dave sat on it last week."

"The legends tell, from what I hear,
That Mother Feakle shall appear
Should this queer amulet but fall
Into the hands of those who call
Themselves her daughters;
Then ladykind shall gain ascendance,
Men made abject in dependence –
I foresee blood and slaughter."

"Yes, well," Jack nodded. "As you say.
Just give's it, we'll be on our way."
He feels a stirring in his grippers.
"Don't think a girlie shall outwit us!"
"It's here," said Fleabag, "In this packet –
Quietly now, don't make a racket."

Goodbyes exchanged, they set off home –
And Barry called "When next you come
Please bring me charts of distant isles,
A good nine inches to the mile!"
After some silence, Bill began:
"Well, wasn't he a *lovely* man!"

Part Five

To Cobblerswood Village in Membershire

Still waiting in bay G,
Kitty sits resignedly;
The bus must come sometime or other
To take her home to her ailing mother;
No point complaining, it made no difference,
She was a thing of little consequence,
And knew it.

In all things meek, passive, compliant –
Why! Here comes Jack and the oafish giant!

The driver of the 46,
Leslie 'Fat Boy' Jeavons,
Cried "All aboard for Cobblerswood,
The Mire and Nether Regions!"

He settled in his burnished seat,
Kicked his wellies from his feet,
Took the money from the throng,
And, pulling out, burst into song:

The Song of Leslie Jeavons

"Oh, give me the life of a travelling man,
And I'll give you a cheery smile!
For it's rickety-tickety-tickety
Every rickety-tickety mile!"

"Yes, climb aboard the big red bus,
You're sure of a safe arrival!
Unless the system grinds to a halt
When I haven't got change of a fiver!"

The bus trembled through Scrote Estate
Where scrawny locals lay in wait,
Devising Leslie Jeavons' fate:
"Let's smear excreta on his pate!"
"Let's hide his glasses!" chortled one –
But then the louts are overcome
By wan dejection and ennui –
"No, let's all just go home for tea."
They felt sad for how they'd behaved
And, as the bus drove by, just waved.

Then once he'd left the stinking town
Jeavons quickly put on speed –
"Must get back before the shop shuts!
There's *some groceries* I need!"
At length he reaches Cobblerswood –
The village shop's still open – "Good!"

Leslie Jeavons

Part Six

A simple mistake puts great power in evil's hands

The passengers climbed down the stairs
And set off home in their threes or pairs;
'Cept Kitty, who stands on her own,
And stares and stares and stares.

"How strange to be a giant –
How strange to be a male –"
She studied Bill and, 'gainst her will,
Thought "Giant legs and giant arms,
Giant smile and giant charm –"
And, with a sense of sweet alarm,
"Is *everything* to scale?"

She turned to wend her way back home
Alone, like oft before;
When, bumping into skulking Jack,
Their bags fell to the floor.

"Sorry, mister," Kitty bends
To pick them from the dog turds, fag ends;
Gives Jack one bag, clasps her own,
By such simple chances are destinies hewn.

"Well, that's all right, love, no harm done,"
Dare she detect a friendly tone?
But no flicker of interest can she trace –
No hidden lust betrays his face –
He' not interested in her sex –
Well, what's a plain girl to expect?
Bags exchanged, he just says "Ta,"
Avoids a passing motor car.

The fairies groan, the fairies cry,
Oh, what a grim catastrophe!
The stupid wanker, what's he done?
He's gone and taken the wrong one!
He's got the single by Dwayne Malone!
She's got the Fogrunt Amulet!
The fairies bowed their heads and wept.

Part Seven

Warnings sound

A long way off, in *The Crooked Crook*,
To the east of Stinchcombe Tap,
Reg Swizell told stories of the zoo –
"I've never seen such elephant crap!
Nor heard such gossip 'mongst the rooks!
There's something wrong in Cloudland –
Something new!"

There was a cough,
A shout,
A ribald laugh,
And conversations carried on.

Reg Swizell

13

Part Eight

Jack and Bill's home improvement

Back at home in their little cottage
Bill exclaimed "I'm fit for dropping!"
"Oh no," said Jack, "Not yet, you won't –
It's your turn to unpack the shopping!"

"I can't be bothered," grumbled Bill, "I'll put it all in there –
The damp and cluttered cupboard that we've got beneath the stairs;
But that rubber lady's thingy's for the dresser by the clock,
We'll gaze upon those lovely parts with every tick and tock.
And when Reverend Scrimp comes calling,
On his rounds next Tuesday morning,
While we're sat and taking tea,
A fine discussion piece she'll be!"

Part Nine

*Back at her family home, Kitty begins to realise
the importance of the amulet*

Along the way, not far away,
The Flaps sat down for tea;
Then went through to the sitting room
To watch some crap TV.

"I like this chap, he makes me laugh,"
Said Dad, all fragile cheer;
"I like the way he doffs his hat
And says *I do feel queer*."

"I like a decent sitcom
That doesn't trade on smut,"
He burbled on, but in that room
There formed a frozen, gloomy, dreadful,
Long-thought, unsaid *But* –
A sense of creeping doom.

It gathered on the china birds
That nestled on the shelf;
It burned inside the TV lamp
And all the 'comic' elves –
That single, sad, unspoken truth:
They were, at once, a family
Yet each one by himself.

"You off out later, love?" Mum asked
The silent, sullen Kitty;
"There's not much going on tonight,"
"Oh dear," said Mum. "A pity."

"I'm going to my room to play
The record what I bought today,"
"That's nice," said Mum;
Said Dad "What's that?
You haven't got money to waste on tat!
You ought to save up for when we
Go with your nan to the caravan
At Thrusting-by-the-Sea."
('Twas there Mum bought an elf each year –
"Another one for your collection, dear?")

Kitty opened her bag and gasped –
What was this within her grasp?
A wondrous sight, enchanting, bright –
It seemed to almost trap the light
Within its silvery clasp.

She stood amazed, enrapt, entranced,
For such a thing she'd never had;
There came a rapping at the door –
"It's your Dad."

Unthinking, Kitty slipped the band
Over her unworldly hand,
And something she'd ne'er understand
Came softly over her.

Dad stomped in to make things clear,
Said "What's all this about, my d..."
Softened, smiled and sidled near,
Came softly close to her.

"You're looking very nice tonight,"
He sat down on the bed;
Too close? Well almost, but not quite –
He looked at her again and said:

"Quite a young lady you've become...
You must have noticed changes...
I've been meaning to talk to you about...
Er...
Um...
Er...
Is that the doorbell?"

Left alone again,
Kitty regarded herself
Coolly in a mirror –
Brushed her hair, brushed her hair,
Brushed her hair;
Dabbed a little *Gypsy*
Here and there, here and there,
Here and there,
Smiled.

"And am I thus translated?"
She mused unto herself;
And with a laugh of triumph
Swept her whimsies from their shelf.

By an eerie force she's overcome,
It captures her whole being;
The room starts spinning round and round –
She's not sure what she's seeing;
Her glossy pic of Dwayne Malone
Is now a vision of a throne.

And on it sits young Kitty Flaps –
"Perhaps... Perhaps...
Perhaps... Perhaps...
I now at last see the *real* me
And recognise my destiny!"

The room it slows and then stands still –
Her gaze rests on the window sill.
"From henceforth any man whose eye
Shall fall upon my breast or thigh
Shall be my faithful drone!
For as Mistress of the Amulet
I need all the dongers I can get
Turned into stone!"

Part Ten

Wizard Dave tells of Cloudland's grim destiny

Grimly over Plumpham Meadows
Rides the firm-jawed Wizard Dave;
With a mind beset by shadows –
Doesn't see the bunnies wave.

A bunny waving

Hurries down the high-banked back lanes,
Cloak drenched by the driving black rain,
Reaches Cobblerswood and, slowing,
Feels a sense of danger growing;
Knocks upon the window pane –
Calls "Jack! It's Wizard Dave!"

"Visited ye old Fleabag?
Got ye the Amulet?"
"Um?" said Jack,
"What's that you ask?
You know, I *quite* forget...
But never mind about that now,
Come in, make yourself comfy,
For there's racing on the telly
And we're going to have a little bet."

Wizard Dave

"The Amulet! *The Amulet!*
Shut up, you dolt, and go and get
The blessed Fogrunt Amulet!
For time is short, now understand
That if that magic band
Should fall into wrong hands
Ere long you'll look in sorrow
Upon your glans."

"Oh, *that* Amulet," said Jack,
"Why didn't you say before?
It's in the cupboard under the stairs
With all the other rubbish there – "
The wizard he thrust Jack aside
And marched toward the cupboard door.

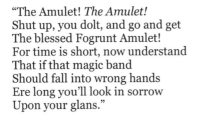

"Two china cocks, stale buns and string...
And what's this underneath?
Some *pants without a gusset* and...
Yee-ughhh! *A funeral wreath!*
But what now of the Amulet?
Please say you kept it on its own!
Ah, yes! A separate paper bag!
What's this? That arse, Malone!"

He turned the single in trembling hands –
"You don't know what you've done!"
Said Bill "We've gone and got that track
That's bound for number one!"

"No!" boomed Dave,
"I'll hear no more!
No more will I hear!
No more!
I have to tell you what is lost
And Cloudland has in store!"

Bill, flopped in an armchair,
Declared "I like a yarn!"
Then discovered that he's sat
In a small, black, icy tarn
That Wizard Dave had conjured with
A wave of his long arm.

"Now, hear ye this and hear ye good –
For Time itself's our foe;
The watch hands wave sarcastically
As round and round they go;
The hourglass has lost her waist –
The sands are all near run;
And sundials gather on the lawns
To snigger at the sun."

And so Dave told them of the Amulet,
Of Kitty Flaps and how
She was born not of woman but
Of a monstrous, hairy, forty-teated
Forest-dwelling sow;
Whose progeny, 'twas writ, would reign
If she that Fogrunt bracelet gained:
A charm made from the finest threads
Of Mother Feakle's golden head.

"And you!" spat Dave,
"You swapped it!
For a palsied balladeer!
A nonce! Poltroon!
A twat! Buffoon!
You've just got no idea!
Oh, the fear! The fear! The fear!"

Said Jack and Bill "Oh dear."

Part Eleven

Manifestations.

And, from that day,
Throughout the land,
The smutty magazines
Showed not big-breasted housewives,
Nor sumptuous well-stacked teens;
For little tits became the thing
For men to feast their eyes on –
And low, flat hills gave them their thrills
When they searched the horizon.

Here Ends Book One

Book Two: A Photo of a Grape

Part One

*At Castle Flowery Dress, King Wobblyknobble ignores
the warnings of a moth*

"My! What a splendid summer's day!
It's just the day to be king!
With not a care in my regal head,
There's nought to do but sing!"

And Wobblyknobble *tra la la'd*
And *fiddle dee'd* and *pooped* and *parped*;
Around the high-walled garden pranced –
"Oh, life's a scrumptious thing!"

"The dewdrops on the hedges wink!
The shrubs are stuffed with birds
Who sing a sweet rejoinder to
My pet wasps' rhythmic whirr!"
(Wob kept wasps 'cos he'd once been told
That they'd make lemon curd.)

King Wobblyknobble

He wittered on for hours on end
Till weariness on him descends;
"Methinks I'll take a little nap!"
He gives his hands a little clap.

From behind a nearby rhododendron
Appeared three maidens fair;
Clad in nought but skimpy slips,
With sensuous, eager rosebud lips –
(They brought a chair.)

They helped him to a nearby arbour
(Staffed by six with a full-time barber)
And at his feet they stoop:
"Would my liege like a bowl of soup?"

"Soup is really *so last year*, you silly little things –
Now kindly bid the gardeners to attend;
I'm sick of all those privet ships
They pruned for me last night –
I want a scene depicting fighting men."

A maiden popped a chocolate-covered thrush into his mouth,
Another peeled a freshly hard-boiled owl;
"The last one in captivity, the Lesser-Bothered Stoop,
Fattened up on naught but Glutton Fowl."

But just as Wob was sizing up a roasted wing of Dox
(A discreetly-titled cross between a white duck and a fox),
A moth flew o'er the garden wall
And settled on his socks.

The king jumped up in great dismay –
His face it turned an ashen grey –
The maids screamed "What's the matter?"
"You know, I've quite gone off this food,
So hurry, dearies, if you could –
I want that moth in batter!"

"Stop what you're doing!" squeaked the moth,
"Stop it, I insist!
It's me, my lord, the brown moth, Blue –"
The king he stayed his fist:
"Send for my expert, Cheeky Pete,
Court lepidopterist!"

"Now hear this well," the moth then warned,
"For once take some advice –
Unless you heed the news I bring
Ere long you'll pay the price!"

Wob called the barber "Over here!
Quick, man! Cover up my ears!
I'll not listen to a word she says –
She's bound to spoil my lovely day –"
He raised his voice, began to sing –
"Sorry, moth, can't hear a thing!"

Blue was a moth, a moth like no other,
Didn't circle the lights like a cork round a drain;
For she loved old King Wob and longed to be his lover,
And lived just to dance in his cold, heedless flame.

She came to rest on the bald bonce
Of this inbred and pampered ponce;
But there's a secret to be told
About this moth, forthright and bold.

She was a fairy in disguise,
By the name of Gossamergonk;
Ashamed of her unsightly thighs
And the pimple on her conk;
Her labial palps all moist with bliss,
She longed for just one royal kiss.

But what cared Wob for real love?
He just didn't give a toss;
The poor, misguided sybarite
Considered love equal to shite –
Surrounded himself by fawning minions,
Glowed when they praised his naff opinions:
"As long as they know who's boss."

"The tides are caused by giant squids
 Expelling noxious ink;
The lower class possess a gene
That causes them to stink;
Rivers run uphill at night,
That's how they keep on going..."
Wob's courtiers all nod their heads:
"Oh, keep the wisdom flowing!"

But all Wob's servants,
And all his knowledge,
All his pride,
And all his privilege,
Couldn't change one stony fact –
Something in his kingdom's cracked.

The moth had sensed this on her travels –
"The fabric of your realm unravels;
I've heard it in the sprouting seeds,
And when the wind blows through the reeds;
Seen it writ in spiders' webs,
And off-white stains in teenage beds;
Something evil's come to town –"

Wob played at quoits with his ancient crown.

Part Two

At the Flaps' house, tea and evil brew

Saturday dawned bright and clear
"Time to get up now, my dear,"
It's Mrs Flaps, stood by a bed,
"Come on! Wake up, Sleepyhead!"
In her hand a cup of tea –
We're going down town, your dad an' me."

Hard indeed to believe the source
Of so much dread, disquiet, anxiety
Lay curled up in a ball beneath
A faded Dwayne Malone duvet –
"I'll leave it on the side – your tea."

"And good luck with your little job,"
Cried Daddy up the stair;
"Today it's just the local shop –
Tomorrow – who knows where?"

The girl fingered the magic charm
Encircling her pasty arm,
Enthralled by its potential
And its power to do great harm.

She moved her hand a little bit
And lay there, gently stroking it.

Part Three

Kitty's Saturday job earns her knowledge of what drives men

Ida Scuttle's little shop was called *The Country Store*,
A fitting name as nine in ten would only go there for
The porno mags she harboured
Upon the highest shelf:
"I can't deny it's self-abuse
That's helped jack up my wealth."

Lady Fromage De La Nobbe
Came in to buy some cakes –
"I'll have two of the eclairs, my dear,
I've just no time to bake..."

"What with all the milking
There's no time these days for fun –
A walnut whip, some jellied snakes,
And that nice cherry bun..."
She casts her eyes on the filthy smut –
Averts her gaze, says "Tut! Tut! Tut!"

Lady Fromage De La Nobbe

Ida measures out some sweets –
"And one more makes a quarter,"
Craftily rests her breast on the scale –
"Do tell me, how's your daughter?"

Next came Mrs Barley-Mow,
A farmer's wife, congealed;
"Have you any dead lambs
We can dump in our top field?"

"I'd like a single hob-nailed boot,
A mattress and a pram;
A tractor tyre, a three-barred fire,
An old clay pot of jam;
For leaving round our wood, you see,
If we're to get our subsidy."

Kitty studied the life of the shop,
Drank every detail in;
But all the time her fascination
Rested on one thing.

She swiftly grasped the power the porn
Had on all the men that morn –
The way they sidled round the aisles,
Feigning interest in the piles
Of dented tins and dated games
Before they dived at their real aim.

Flat Girls, Thin Girls, Nice'n'Small–
Poor Bob the Hare peered at them all;
But not a big jug could he find:
"It's just not natural," he opined.

Nympho, Desperate, Readers' Pets –
"The other day I was at the vet's..."
Cloudland Babes and Liver Fun –
"Why must you eat it upstairs, son?"

The Sexy World of Men Called Keith –
"Luckily I'd rinsed me teeth..."
Each wrapped inside a greaseproof bag
Marked 'This contains a dirty mag'.

Part Four

*The sins of the village menfolk find them
out and Kitty finds new strength*

Fresh from a meeting of the Parish Council
("A sterling group of men,")
The Reverend Scrimp peers through the door –
"Ahem, ahem, ahem."

"Such lovely tins! A pack of cards
To mark Wob's coronation!"
But all the time his eyes strayed to
Home and Masturbation.

He stood there by the magazines,
Flicking through the pages
Of *Rural Walks Through Membershire*
And *Knitting Patterns Through the Ages;*
Yet more and more he found himself
Being drawn towards the topmost shelf.

The Reverend Godfrey Scrimp

And as he sweated, shifted, sighed,
Kitty felt a change inside –
As though his power it ebbed her way
With every impure thought that day.

He stands, he shakes with indecision,
"But what about my reputation?"
What would be the thoughts of his congregation
If they caught him with *Dirty Domination*?
If they knew that their money from this week's collection
Had been spent on the latest *Maintain Your Erection*?
Or what would they say if he walked past their gardens
With shiny new copies of *Spank Me* and *Hard On*?
And how would she view him? This girl with no bust –
If he purchased an edition of *Old Man's Lust?*

At last he snatched at *Naughty Frills*
And slapped it by the till;
"Just for my friend, you understand...
He's recently died... He's ill."

As Kitty fumbled with his change,
Scrimp stared up at the ceiling –
Then he took a peek down her starched white top
And felt the strangest feeling.

He hurries home –
Checks he's all alone,
Confronts the fact that, somehow,
His dong has turned to stone.

Mrs Scuttle's round the back
(Giving her husband a quick whack)
And Kitty's left to mind the shop;
She feels her inner power growing,
The force of life is overflowing –
"Oh! Take me! Take me! Please don't stop!"

Part Five

Jack and Bill consort with complacency

Ida Scuttle

Angry voices echo 'cross the green in Cobblerswood,
Angry voices bouncing off the eaves;
"First he turns my chair into a small, black, icy tarn,
Then he does his nut an' fuckin' leaves."

"Who does he think he is?" asked Jack,
"And what gives him the right?
Barging in here just like that?
It really spoiled my night!"

Bill he teased their parrot
With a photo of a grape;
"I hate it when these wizard blokes
Drop by to just go ape."
"I can't see why this amulet
Is such a priceless thing;
Has he never heard 'Jive Man' Malone
Play the spoons and sing?"

"We got a bargain there,
It's been at number one for ages;
It's easily the best he's done
Since his last, *Can't Turn the Pages*."

And Bill he danced a foxtrot
With his shadow on the wall;
"Oh, do keep time!" he barked at it,
"And try to stand up tall!
Oh, why, whenever I draw close
D'you shrink and get so small?"

Part Six

Wizard Dave visits the Flaps to retrieve Kitty's treasure

Threading through suburban hedges
Stalks a figure black and grey;
Past the ranks of twelve-foot wedges,
Gardens owners hoped would say
"We're tidy folk, just keep away."

The figure stops at thirty-four,
This is the house he's searching for,
This is the one where *evil* lies;
He stands before the Flaps' front door,
And pauses to adjust his flies.

Behind the door they've had their tea,
The dishes done and put away;
"Now, best go do your homework, love,
What have you got today?"
"Only sums, it's not too bad,"
"Well, best set to it," "Okay, Dad."

Mum's started on the ironing,
Holds up a pair of aged pants –
"These'll not see much more wear,
You can't leave things to chance!"

Dad's settled in his favourite chair,
Sleeveless jumper, thinning hair;
He's looking forward to his shows –
He'll take his socks off, pick his toes –
Around the room he casts an eye –
Thinks "What a splendid man am I."

But, what's this? It's the door bell
A-ringing in the hall –
He looks accusingly at mum
"Are *you* expecting anyone?
It's *far* too late to call!"

When he opens up the door
And finds a wizard there
Flaps he almost slams it shut
To block that brooding stare.

Wizard Dave stands, faltering,
Darts at Flaps a cheesy grin,
Peers beyond him up the stair –
Senses magic treasure there –
"Is Kitty in?"

Mr Flaps

This was the moment Flaps had feared,
Flaps had feared for all these years;
The moment when *the gentlemen*,
Slick gentlemen, sly gentlemen,
Laid siege to Kitty's sex –
"The war's begun."

And even as he shook Dave's hand
And felt his age-hewn skin,
He thought of what these fingers sought
And where they'd soon be in.

An uninvited image came –
Another that he dared not name –
His daughter, taking off her shirt;
This Dave, his hand up Kitty's skirt.

He strove to drive from out his mind
His daughter, on all fours;
This bearded chancer close behind,
Rummaging through her drawers.

Again the paintings in the attic
Of his troubled brain
Showed naught but lurid pictures
That pulsed inside their frames.

He saw a pair of spindly crabs
Run across white sands;
Thought of those old and wizened claws
Upon her mammary glands.

Dave essayed a question –
"I wonder if I might...?"
"I'll bet you do, you filthy swine!
I've got you bang to rights!"

"You wonder if you *what*, my lad?
Defile my little girl?
Bury your ugly, lusting face
Deep in those golden curls?"
(Transported, Dad was unaware
He'd mounted the back of a nearby chair.)

In spite of all his brave attempts
To banish all these thoughts
They still aroused him *just a bit*,
He felt a stirring in his shorts.

Dave resolved to set things straight
"Calm yourself now, please!
I simply want to see your girl –
She's something that I need!"

"You people!" spluttered Mr Flaps –
"You come here to my home
With all your *sex* and *filth* and *sex* –
Just please leave us alone!"
He slammed the door and turned away
To face the rest of his hollow days.

The wizard, in the garden,
Stands among Dad's prize carnations;
He sees a light that's on upstairs,
A silhouetted figure there,
Wrongly balancing equations.

"Just how to get at her?" he asked,
"Without that awful man!"
Nonplussed by this old fool's rebuttal
He thinks "I'll have to be more subtle –
Next time I'll try her Nan."

Part Seven

The men of Cobblerswood Council discuss a very local problem

Tuesday night, 8p.m.,
The parish rooms:
The babble of grievance and counter-grievance:
The sounds of men
Bent on matters of great importance.

"I want to know just when the council
Plans to sort these leaves
That clutter up my lawn each year?
Does Cobblerswood *need* trees?"

Godfrey Scrimp smiled benignly
From the Treasurer's chair:
"Thank you, Mr Heckmondwyke,
"It's in the council's care."

Piped up builder Terry Spratt
"Well, there's another matter that
Demands hasty decision;
Concerning Widow Frottage
And her rose-strewn, thatched-white cottage,
Why can't you just agree to knock it down?"

Councillor Smethurst raised a hand –
At once the floor went quiet;
He didn't say "Still your prattle,
You jumped-up handyman,"
But his poached-egg eyes implied it.

"Mr Spratt... Terry... Tel...
I think we know each other well,
I think you'll know my meaning when I say –
Permission's in the bag, old friend,
As long as you keep up your end
And visit Mrs Smethurst every day."

Councillor Smethurst

"And then you'll have your new estate
Where Fogrunt's overflow can go;
The village locksmith just can't wait,"
Said 'Fingers' Gifford, smiling, "No."

29

Then Fishman Grundy held the floor,
The rest looked on in silence.
He'd come along this evening for
Renewal of his annual licence
To sell his fish from door-to-door
And stop and have a blether;
Though people counted him a bore
(His lips had once been sewn together
By good King Wob for talking bollocks)
He gestured, grunted, tugged his forelock –
"Fine," said Scrimp. "Yes, it shall be,
Now, please, let's move on. AOB?"

At length the meeting reached its close,
Just one more thing determined:
That Farmer Barley-Mow was free
To shoot at kids as vermin.

Scrimp hurried to the toilet,
"If I don't go soon I'll burst..."
But, arriving there, found Baldy King,
Getting out his smelly thing,
"Don't worry, you go first."

Water dripped from the cistern:
Plink
Plink
Plink
"It's been quite mild of late," said Scrimp,
"Don't you think?"

Water dripped from the cistern:
Plink
Plink
Plunk
"The thing is, Reverend, I can't go,
No matter what I've drunk."

"I'm frightened, Rev, I'm so alone,
For something down below has grown
Unnatural, horrid, and unknown..."
Sighed Scrimp "Your dick has turned to stone."

Young Baldy blushed "How can you tell?
This last week's been a living hell!"
Scrimp just shrugged and pointed –
"Me as well."

"I haven't been the same since I
Went shopping for some... Some supplies,"
"Well, I'll -" cried King, "That's just like me!"
"So," came a voice, "We now are three."

Smethurst stood at the next door stall –
"I cannot piss, nothing at all!
I'm slowly going up the wall –
It happened at the shop, I'm sure,
That's when I had some thoughts impure –
To that young girl my strength it poured."

"You'd better make that over thirty,
We all did wrong by feeling dirty,"
Leslie Jeavons led a queue
Of all the village menfolk who
Fate and fanny art had lured.

"It happened when the girl bent down
To get the rubber bands;
I caught the merest, chancest glimpse
Of her lovely mammary glands."

"Down the neck of her chastely-buttoned blouse –
In spite of myself I got aroused –
It's been so lonely round the house
Since Ethel died."

"She looked at me in such a way –
Her cold, grey eyes, they seemed to say
"I know" –
And then I hardened down below."

Part Eight

Kitty's malevolence claims another victim

Back in her bedroom Kitty worked
To extirpate all trace
Of childishness –
She tore a dress,
And drew a moustache on the face
Of singing hunk 'Jive Man' Malone,
Trimmed her soft toys to the bone,
Binned her fun-fur pencil case.

Out the back she built a pyre,
Laughed to see her childhood burn;
Fetched rabbit Nibbles from his hutch,
Sneered "And now it's your turn!"
Danced naked round the fire and then
Chanted a hymn of hating men.

Spying cross the garden wall
Her next-door neighbour watched this all –
The mangy ne'er-do-well, Jim Rix,
On piled–up flowerpots and bricks.

"Miss Flaps has got a fine round bottom!"
He fumbled with his trouser buttons –
But then he gasped, there's something wrong –
He grasped his ossifying dong.

Jim Rix

Part Eight

The Forest of the Skull

Look now upon Cobblerswood,
Look upon the world;
Look upon a great dark wood
Where evil lies their curled.

It is the monstrous, forty-teated
Black and evil sow;
Who suckled infant Kitty Flaps
And lies there, stinking, now.
While questions buzz around like flies:
What next? What if? and *How?*

Here Ends Book Two

Book Three: The Pixie's Magic Log

Part One

Sunlight and shadows

Gallumphing down the valley-o,
Plumping up the trees,
Spinning in a paper boat,
And fattening the breeze –
Summer comes to Cobblerswood,
Lies panting in the wheat,
And every creature seeks a way
To flee the sullen heat.

Some they seek out shady dells
And lie there, pleasuring themselves –
Keeping out a watchful eye
For nymphs and fairies dancing by.

Others go behind closed doors
And keep their curtains shut;
They stay there till it's gone September,
Yanking on their blistered member,
Dehumanised by smut.

Part Two

The Flaps leave for the coast

"Elbow grease and a jaunty whistle!
This'll get the job done –
This'll make the car run –
Never cease till the windows glisten!
Winking back at the sun!"

Mr Flaps was polishing his motor car
In preparation for the summer break:
"A caravan in Thrusting-by-the-Sea, you know,
With crazy golf and a mini boating lake!"

For weeks on end old Flaps had bragged
Each time Jim Rix he'd met:
"The park's got its own billiards room
And a little launderette!"
His neighbour, eyes ablaze with hate,
Had shrugged "Yeh, well, whatever, mate."

"Come, come, now girls, no time to waste –
We must be on our way –
Before the Fogrunt rush hour starts –
We're off! Hip hip hooray!"

He gives his horn a quick toot! toot!
"With patient care I've planned the route –
We've to head towards the A54,"
In the back Nan starts to snore –
Kitty whines "Life's such a bore!"
Nan farts.

They round the first corner, Dad cries out
"Are we nearly there?
You always used to say that, Kit –
Are we nearly there?"

"Oh, yes!" said Mum. "Every year!
Are we nearly there?"
"I was younger then," said Kitty,
"Young with stupid hair!
Stupid clothes and childish shoes
And stupid underwear!"
"Still," said Dad, "You've got to laugh!
Are we nearly there?"

Part Three

*At the Cobblerswood parish rooms,
the guest speaker disappoints*

Each Thursday night they gather here,
The Feakle Maidens of Berloon –
Ladies, tight-lipped and austere,
(Widow Frottage books the room) –
They sit now, waiting patiently
As nears the twilight gloom –
Dolly Felch frets anxiously –
"I hope he gets here soon."

Overmaiden, Mrs Smethurst,
Checks her watch and frowns –
"It's not like Reverend Godfrey Scrimp
To ever let us down."

Mrs Smethhurst

He promised us a talk at eight
On mastering the flesh,
Written after many years abroad –
Based upon the teachings of reformed transsexual 'Ken' –
Written after many years a broad."

34

What Mrs Smethurst didn't see
Was Reverend Scrimp behind a tree –
Trousers round his ankles,
Yanking furiously.

Though his implement's been turned to stone,
Still he can't leave it alone –
And though it now takes ten times longer,
He squeezes pleasure from his donger.

The vicar leant his furrowed brow
Against the furrowed tree:
"I wish, I wish, I wish I knew
What just came over me!"
Said Donny Stoat, wiping his coat,
"I heartily agree!"

He'd set off from the vicarage
With plenty of time to spare –
His notes collated, organised,
Selected all his favourite slides –
But never *quite* got there.

He meandered home uncertainly –
Made some tea –
Couldn't decide
Between two lumps or three.

Mrs Smethurst banged a gavel:
"I think it's time for the sodding raffle!"

Part Four

Our heroes fiddle while Cloudland burns

Jack stood by the dresser.
"I remember this from school –
See, there's the labium minus,
And there's the vestibule!"

"There's care in every detail!
She's so pleasing to the eye!
You hold the lips like that –
And see! The cervix uteri!"

"Next time we're in Fogrunt we
Must buy another two or three
And then she'll have some company –
She looks so lonely by herself
With just my mum's old dildo
On the shelf."

Bill was standing by the window,
Frowning at a sight
That seemed to him to somehow be
Not quite right.

"Baldy King is hovering
Outside *The Country Store* –
He's pressed his knob against the glass
At least three times or more!
Yet still he doesn't enter –
He's bent to tie his shoe –
But he's wearing his brown slip-ons –
Now what's he trying to do?"

Part Five

At Bumming's Caravan Park, the Flaps are thrown together and apart

The Flaps sweep into Thrusting
(Twinned with Dysentery and Mange)
Turn into the track down to the site;
Rattle o'er the goblin grid and
Pass beneath a sign that says
We guarantee our staff will serve you right!

The caravan's Dad's pride and joy,
His little home away from home –
He used to come here as a boy
And up and down the coastline roam,
Clutching his workbook *I Spy Jobbies* –
Every boy must have his hobbies.

Through Paradise he makes his slow
And solitary way:
"Ah, here's the crazy golf course
Where my dad and I would play!"

"Oh, how I fought to win his love –
To be the perfect son –
To putt his heart around and round,
And score a hole in one."

"My father was a hard man,
And difficult to reach –"
"We've heard it all before," said Mum,
"Now let's go to the beach."

That night, tired after a long day,
The dishes done and put away,
The Flaps decide it's time to play:
Dad pipes up "Who's for a game?"
Kitty sneers in cold disdain:
"I'll sit this out if it's all the same."

The others try a game of Snap!
But Nan keeps shouting "Twat!"
And so they are reduced to flicking
Cards into a hat.

Cramped confinement, close conditions –
Sore, uncomfortable positions,
There's barely room to stand in here –
Nan's farts hang heavy in the air,
Dad's halitosis turns his beer.

The picture of ill humour,
Kitty mopes there in the corner –
Broody, sulky and withdrawn –
Cursing the day that she was born.

Dad looked up and shook his head –
"Now, what's got into her?
She used to be the nicest girl,
Polite, without a care –
But recently, oh, I don't know –
Why must our children always grow?"

From the far side of the park
Strange lights twinkle in the dark –
It's the nightly *Teen Scene* disco –
"Mum! Dad! Nan! Please can I go?"
As one the adults answer "No!"

"It's bedtime soon!"
"It's far too late!"
"There might be kids
From Scrote Estate!"

Mrs Flaps she yawns and said
"Well, I'm done in, folks, time for bed!"
The lights go out and Kitty tries
To ignore all the stifled cries
Of pleasure, and the muffled moans,
The grunts, the snuffling, and the groans
That come from where her parents lie,
She wishes she could die.

Nan Flaps

Part Six

*At Merryweather Farm, Jack witnesses more evidence that
change is afoot*

Six a.m. –
Cobblerswood –
Farmer Barley–Mow –
Standing in his bottom field
Where ne'er a rook nor crow
Nor cat nor bat
Nor pygmy shrew
Would ever, ever go.

His gun is cocked,
He bellows "Pull!"
And points the 12 bore high –
As his devoted wife sets two
Clay toddlers in the sky.

His finger tenses on the trigger,
When he espies a far-off figure –
Distant now but getting bigger –
A boy!
Heading for his apple trees –
He aims the shotgun at the knees –
Thunders "Hoy!"

Little Tommy Makepeace

It's little Tommy Makepeace,
He's bagged him twice before –
His rump is leaded
Like a church's roof;
And yet he finds he cannot fire,
And slowly drops the gun:
Shoots a nearby goat
But spares the youth.

The farmer stands there, all confound
Mrs Barley-Mow's astounded –
"How can I hurt a little child?
Or cripple him for life?
So pure, untainted, undefiled?"
"Blimey," says his wife.

Now, by the twisted will of fate,
Our hero Jack espied the scene;
As he lay in a ditch, his bed for the night –
A-drinking he had been.

Mrs Barley-Mow

He turned to last night's conquest –
They'd met on his way home –
And found she had a head of straw,
A body made of foam –
"Ah well," said Jack, "A shag's a shag,
It beats a night alone."

Through bleary eyes and stinging nettles
His gaze upon the farmyard settles –
He sees old Barley-Mow repenting,
He sees the billy goat fall dead;
He sees young Tom Makepeace repenting,
He sees this all and shakes his head.

"There's something strange here, not quite right,"
Turns to his lady of the night –
"I tell you, love, it's downright queer,"
And takes her roughly from the rear.

Part Seven

Mr Flaps suggests a daytrip to Castle Flowery Dress; Kitty is oddly keen

Ah! The tang of creosote!
The zing of shared facilities!
The honest stench of chemical lavs!
Dad sucks it in.

The sense of wartime solidarity –
A burden self-imposed but stoically borne –
Lives laid out for perusal like market stalls –
Dad sucks it in.

Towel thrown over his shoulder
Like some dashing cavalier –
Washing kit tucked under arm –
He tries hard not to peer
At the goblin pissing in a trough –
He doesn't want to look a puff.

A toad steps naked from the shower,
A pixie from the bog;
It's Dad's turn next and there he finds
The pixie's left a magic log;
A bunny rabbit cleans his teeth,
A badger rinses last night's sheath.

Back at his little 'palace on bricks'
Dad makes a packet meal;
A tasty, hot risotto,
With *chunks of genuine veal.*

The badger

39

Outside Kitty plays a solo,
Listless swingball game;
Taking one side, then the next,
With precious little aim.

At length, and in a manner
That she barely understands,
One side of that private feud
Assumes the upper hand.

Her anti-clockwise slashes
Now blast the ball around –
And widdershins, contrary-wise,
Dark victory is found.

"Fly around your orbit,
You stupid little sphere –
See how a flick of my godly wrist
Controls your every year!"

The kettle whistles, tea is made,
The Flaps sit down to eat;
"Now then, I thought this afternoon
I'd give you all a treat!"

"How about a..." started Mum –
"No, that costs too much cash!
I'd thought we might go for a spin –
Try and take the castle in –
Who knows, we'll maybe see the king!
What does Nan think? Sound like fun?"
Nan sucked risotto through her straggly 'tache.

Kitty's snidey mouth falls open,
The spoon she toys with drops.
The strangest look comes over her
She quivers from her ankle socks –
"Yes, I'd like that very much!
I think you're just the tops!"

She leans her head against Dad's vest –
A touching moment, yet,
With her hands behind her back
She strokes the Amulet.

Mrs Flaps

"Now, Kitty, just a word before we go, my dear –
It's something that I really need to know, my dear –
If we see the king, will you promise me one thing,
Will you act your best and always curtsey low, my dear?"

40

And Mum reminded Kitty of her recent errant ways:
Moodiness, attention seeking, cheek –
"And what was all that business when we went to Fogrunt Town
To buy your Dad's new flip-flops just last week?"

"Your father wouldn't like the way
You flirted with those chaps –
There must have been near forty by the end!
They gathered round like Pomfrey Hounds
Who've got a whiff of cress –
A most unsatisfactory group of men!"

"Just not the right sort for my daughter –
A lot were from the Wise Man Quarter –
Wizards, warlocks, and the like,
And a naked monk on a Kingpin bike!"

Part Eight

*Drinking in The Hunter's Hanky, our heroes
don't notice an anxious observer*

"You should've seen her go, mate!
She'd got tits as big as buckets, mate!
I never caught her name, but
We were at it half the night, mate!
And still, this bird, she wanted more – "
"What's that?" asked Bill, "It looks like straw!"

Jack sups his pint –
Narrows his eyes –
Intones
"I saw a sight today
That I..."

He sups his pint –
Clears his throat –
Intones
"I saw a sight today
That chilled my crooked bones."

Jack lowered his voice,
Cast a furtive glance around the snug –
"I've been wondering of late..."
He addressed the rug.

"Some words of Wizard Dave's keep coming
Back to me, back to me..."
He said, his face now looking old;
Something about an Amulet and Destiny –
Is it me,
Or is this room gone sudden cold?"

41

Bill stopped flipping his beer mat
Into his giant hand –
Spoke:
"You're right, little bloke –
I've noticed things I don't understand –
Perhaps old Dave will tell us more –
But it's a week since I last saw
That ragged cloak."

"No, quite," said Jack –
"You're right," said Jack,
"He's been here less and less –
He's gone to stay, he said, I'm sure,
With his aunt, for a walking tour
Of antiquarian sex shops in the west."

Jack's words slowly slipped away,
Dripped into the beer slops tray;
Echoed in an empty mug,
Trickled in that quiet wee snug,
Came to rest in one man's ear –
For Wizard Dave was skulking near.

In a darkened nook close by,
Out of sight of prying eyes,
He'd rather not be recognised,
That's why he travelled in disguise.

A different tie, a trilby hat
(His mother'd find him hard to tell),
Not happy leaving it at that,
He's gone and trimmed his pubes as well.

Yet there he was, sat listening in,
Keeping an eye out, eavesdropping,
And mulling over each word said,
In case it concerned the Dong Maid.

A thankless task for the poor chap
As by and large folk just talked crap:
Stunted peasants, men who glared,
Or vacantly just stood and stared,
Large women with tree-trunk legs,
Foregathered here were Cloudland's dregs.
Hunched exchanges, violent threats,
Tattooed hags with unpaid debts,
Were all here at *The Hunter's Hanky*
(Proprietor one Rowland Twanky).

Strange abuse and filthy rituals
Recur each day in this grim shithole –
Disturbed to hear his name thus spoken,
Dave girds his loins, grabs his beer tokens,
Pulls his hat down o'er his snout
And hurries out.

Bill went to the bar and bought
Eleven packs of nuts,
Hoping that each purchase would
Reveal a bit more smut.

For they were pinned to a picture
Of D-Cup in the buff.
"Oh, please can I have that other pack?
The one that hides her chuff!"

Jack joined him, looking happier now –
"I've got a good idea!
Why don't we visit Fleabag?
I'm sure he'll quell our fears –
The bus leaves at a quarter past, –
We'll catch it if we're fast..."

At a quarter to the pair still wait –
"The bus to Fogrunt's always late!"
But this one never comes at all –
At home Jeavons stared at the wall –
Slumped in a chair with lumpy pants:
"I can't be bothered... Can't be... Can't..."

Granny D-Cup

Part Nine

Kitty gains the throne room and good King Wob is caught short

Parp, parpetty parp!
Parpetty, parp parp parp
PARP!

A fusillade of trumpet song
Comes blasting from the walls –
A thousand pikestaffs stand in serried ranks –
The whole display's an exercise
In saying to the proles
"We're strong, you're weak,
Please don't forget it, thanks."

The Flaps cross the drawbridge cautiously,
Are somewhat taken aback to see
The great main gate manned by one soul –
A chap in a cap with a badge marked *Noel* –
He finds a family ticket in his shed –
"Now see the guide – his badge says *Fred*."

Mum hovers round the teacloths
Emblazoned with heraldic crests;
Dad's lost interest, stands and stares
At a passing woman's breasts.

Nan's just lost in wonder
At the splendour of the hut;
They're happy playing out their role
Of docile peasants, but...

But where is Kitty? Where is she now?
She's wandered off again!
A worry line creases Mum's brow,
Dad sidles off to find the men's.

Sighs Mum "Now, where's she got to?
It's really got to stop!
She thinks of no one but herself –
Well, I'm off to the tea shop!"

Nan nods and smiles,
And coughs and splutters –
But no one hears
The words she utters.

Kit's slipped beneath a velvet rope
But takes no time to stop and gawp
Ignores a sign that says 'Keep out'
A sentry sees her, gives a shout.

"Hoy! Stop, young miss!' the sentry cries,
She offers him a flash of thigh;
He feels an ossifying thrill –
"Come, this away, Madam, if you will!"

The soldier feels his growing ardour,
Growing ardour, growing ardour.
Cracks appear upon his armour,
How his codpiece strains!
The metal warps, contorts and struggles,
Chainmail bucks and bends and buckles,
Kitty gives a callous chuckle;
Now the male is chained!

Noel

While he stares at her pasty skin
Young Kitty spies a side door in;
It's brightly-lit and strewn with rugs,
The Amulet it pulls and tugs.

In the throne room with his courtiers,
Greeting visitors of state,
A movement in the royal derriere
Hails the need to defecate.

So there formed a grand procession
To oversee the king's excretion,
More pained, more pained grew his expression
The closer it drew near.

It's pressing on his rectal walls
As they proceed through the Great Hall;
As one the servants raise a shout:
"Make way! The king must squeeze one out!"

Meantime, something in the throne room's changed,
Yes, something's strange,
As if that musty cube of air
Is one held breath;
As if the chairs
Have stiffened, stand now to attention,
Silent as the guards of death.

Why, Kit's ensconced upon the throne!
She'd waited till the king was gone –
"They'll notice *now*," was all she said;
The amulet burned fiery red.

At this the toilet cracked in two,
Wob's arse-wipe knew not what to do
And scarpered through the nearby door
While the king squirmed upon the floor;
He'd never learned to wipe himself,
"Assistance, please!" he shrilly yelped.

His entourage recoils in fear,
They run away, the counts and lords;
Outraged, King Wob bursts into tears –
"You'll all be sorry, mark my words!"

He's helped up by a bandy wench
Who holds her nose to block the stench;
She then applies the quilted sheet,
Her joy's sublime! Her life's complete!

That she, a menial, low and humble,
Elsie Muck of Bumblybumble,
Should have her fingers in *his* shits!
Her grandpa would be thrilled to bits!

Wob looks at her with grateful eye,
The soil gone from his upper thigh;
"A thousand thanks! I shan't forget
Your hand upon my intergluteal cleft."

And then he did a pique-filled dance
Till the wench fetched his other pants;
He scolded her "Go, get a broom!"
Then stomped off back to the throne room.

Elsie Muck

But hang on - *What! How could this be?*
A teenage girl was in his place!
She lounged there with authority,
She had flat tits and a dull face.
The king was outraged: "By my beard!
What gym-slip queen awaits me here?"

The young pretender smiled,
Paused a while
Then deigned to speak.
If, indeed, pretence it was
Then none could seek
A finer actor for this stage.
"Why, here's the king of far-off days!"
"Old man, depart! Get from my sight!
For I am queen now, by birth right!
Begone for ever! Don't come back!"
Wob urged three soldiers to attack –
But then she showed them all her gash –
Then thunder roared and lightning flashed.

More soldiers came and, likewise awed
By Kitty's flesh, all drew their swords
And dragged Wob to the castle's gate –
He spluttered "I protest! No! Wait!
Stay, men, and let me back inside!
You can't do this! It's regicide!
She shall be punished, wait and see!
She shall be spanked across my knee!"

A mob had gathered, wildly braying,
None heard a word the king was saying –
He cried out "Take me back! You must!"
But was cast into the dust.

The mob leered at him, cruelly, meanly –
"We want this girl, for she's more queenly!"
They kicked and spat at him obscenely –
(We'll draw a veil, for it's unseemly.)

Yet one bald servant, faithful, trusty,
With scissors gone all blunt and rusty,
Followed Wob in all his shame –
Old Dick the Barber was his name.

Quiet now!
Quiet.
Quiet as the elves
Who pad along the moss-ways
In the wood.

Can you hear the clanging of the bluebells,
Of the bluebells,
Tolling for the end of all things good?

A revolting subject

Some children play at conkers on the Clumbolt Heath,
But rabbit skulls are hanging from their strings.
A seamstress pricks her finger on a churchyard bench,
A plumber climbs a tree and starts to sing.

And so it was that when night came,
Moon was hoisted up its flagpole,
All of Cloudland saw a change
In that pale face,
The centre now was but a hole
And round it just a gleaming trace;
A circle like an amulet
Of portents dark and power strange.

Part Ten

Pig in mud

And all the while the monstrous
Hairy, forty-teated sow
Lies squirming on her back in porcine glee –
Nipples bright as glow-worms,
One burning twice as strong,
Lighting up the cradling canopy.

Here ends Book Three

Book Four: The Horses of My Hands

Part One

The talk of Fogrunt

"And then there's my Bert," the one began.
"With the pains," the other replied.
"Last week he left them by the coal shed –
This week he's put them by the clothes horse."
"All down his left–hand side."

A robin landed at the feet
Of these two ladies on the street,
Who clutched their handbags to their chests
As though their leather depths possessed
Some distillation of their lives
As maidens, sweethearts, women, wives.

"And robins aren't what they used to be."
"No, they're shorter."
"They're somehow not as robiny."
"How *is* your daughter?"

"What d'you make of that new one?"
"What one?"
"That one with the bones –"
"Why ever did she wear that red
When she's got a purple throne?"

"Well, it's been lovely." "Lovely, yes."
"We'll do it again soon."
And, shopping bags picked up, they fled
Into the busy afternoon.

Part Two

In The Great Depression, Wobblyknobble languishes in exile

Mean of spirit, black of look,
Behold a broken wanderer stoop
Nearby a filthy, stinking brook
And dream of bowls of soup.

And oh! What a paltry retinue
This once proud soul now leads;
A donkey shod in carpet slippers,
One servant armed with nought but clippers,
They sit amongst the reeds.

"How low we've fallen!" his plaintive cry–
"Tossed by cruel Fortune's tides!"
"And what'll it be today, my lord?
A nice short back and sides?"

Have ever the tonsorial arts been practised
In such a dismal spot?
Probably not.

This was the River Sluggard
That slid across the land,
Parting the cold and clammy banks
Like a delving pervert's hands.

Sluggard had crawled for a hundred miles
To reach that tableau sad;
Lugubrious and sour as if
It wondered why it had.

"I chuckled as I tumbled
Out from the Hills of Steve,
And frolicked over Plumpham Vale,
Was sad I had to leave."

"I lingered in the cress fields,
Was asked to stay to tea;
But all the time the Nether Regions
Kept on calling me."

"And now I have traversed those lands
And reached the other side –
Where lies The Great Depression
That's as long as it is wide."

Leaning on a knotted stick
The wanderer moans "I am quite sick!
Banished! Never more to see
My people gaze adoringly –
Come close, my faithful Barber Dick!"

"Of course you'll still be, being banished!
But good to see your dandruff's vanished!
Would you like to see the back?"
Dick turned him round on his piece of sack.

Old Dick

Part Three

A gathering at Fleabag Barry's receives an unwelcome royal visitor

The apothecary's lair was shut,
A sign said 'Gone to Seed';
"Gone to seed?" young Jack did read –
"It seems deserted but
I sense there's something there inside,"
With trembling hand the door he tried –
"Come, Bill, and take the lead!"

They fumbled darkly round the back
Of Fleabag Barry's wooden shack –
Bill peered through the curtains' chink,
Quickly turned away in fright;
"There's a meeting going on, I think,
We'd best come back another night."

Fleabag's back room, dank and black room,
Filled with thirty-nine of those whom
Kitty Flaps had kept in thrall
With just a hint of minge,that's all.

Troubled looks and shame-faced glances,
Men who'd thought they'd take their chances,
Who'd told themselves they'd all be all right,
Their deeds now held up to the light,
Exposed as wankers every one –
Regretting things they'd often done.

These grotty men of every class
Who loved to ogle teenage arse
Of every profession and trade
Who longed to see girls' breasts displayed
They're not so bold now that they're here –
They're frightened, nervous, chilled with fear
As Bernard Smethurst, with a groan,
Uplifts his voice and starts to moan:

"Kitty, Kitty, Kitty, Kitty!
Kitty, Kitty, Kitty, Kit!
We've not deserved your bounteous pity,
Sorry that we've been so shitty,
We all think you're really pretty,
Kitty, Kitty, Kitty!"

Incorporeal voices scream,
It's like some madman's anguished dream,
Unearthly light transforms the gloom –
And Kitty's form's there in the room.

She's come and answered their behest!
(They know it's her, she's got no chest) –
Transported by the Amulet's power
From Flowery Dress to Fleabag's Bower –
She laughs with a malicious sneer
At all the men who're gathered here;
And in a voice cold, mean and grim,
Begins:

"As I gaze around this room,
Your ugly, upturned faces
Take me back to suburb scrub,
And scrag-end, brownfield places,
And those few sad, surviving flowers
That ring the unmown lawns,
As if still waiting for the one
Who'd tend them every morn.

For now I know you'd like to learn
What drives your new-crowned queen
To persecute your shrivelled sex,
Regress towards the mean!

Part Four

Queen Kitty tells of her past and the ghastly future for Cloudland's men

I was abandoned as a small tot,
Discarded inside an old
Box swaddled in a dirty loin cloth,
Left out in the dark and cold.

I might have lain for days, perhaps,
Ere being found by Mrs Flaps,
Who gave a startled cry of joy –
How wonderful! A little boy!

She couldn't have kids of her own,
She'd difficulties ovulating;
But there she saw me all alone,
On her door step, just freezing, waiting.

I picked me from where I'd been laid
And took me in to meet a man,
"Behold, your child," was all she said,
Then handed me to Nan.

The man turned green at this suggestion,
Mrs Flaps asked "Not well, Dear?
A little touch of indigestion?"
"No, I'm feeling not 'alf queer."

Nan brought out a crocheted rug
For me, the helpless little nestling,
She belched, then farted, gave a shrug,
Went back in to watch the wrestling,
Muttering something as she went,
No one could tell, though, what she meant.

I grew to call them Mum and Dad
And Nan (who slept beneath the stairs);
They named me Kitty for their cat,
And raised me as if I was theirs.

I always felt a special bond
Between my dad and me;
He'd walk me round the local pond
And dandle me upon his knee.

He sang a little lullaby
About a piggy in a wood –
It made me sad and want to cry,
Though why I never understood;
He sang it while he tucked me in,
I almost felt like we were kin.

Things were different with Mum, who
Had lady's problems 'down below'
Which made her very sensitive –
And quite a challenge to live with;
She spent most of my childhood sick,
And always made me empty it.

Then one dark day, still innocent,
And playing at explorers,
I found behind a 'keep out' sign
Dad's secret bottom drawer.

Toffees, tampons, underwear,
A dish of fresh-plucked nasal hairs,
A rubber glove, some creams and lubes,
A toupee made from his own pubes –
There at the back, a plastic mac
With neatly cut-out holes,
And magazines that lay between
Its damp and greasy folds.

It's Not Illegal, Keep Her Keen,
A Woman's Place is on My Cock,
Misogyny and Puzzle Time,
Coprophile, My Favourite Sock.

Buttock Fun and *Slap My Thighs,*
Piano Slut and *Muffled Cries* –
(A contact mag for guys who care:
"Got a care home? We'll be there!")

Sauce and *Pants Off, Gentlemen!*
Lick My Bell End Now and Then,
Bleeding, Up Yours, Deep Regret,
Bend Over, Please and *Our Secret.*

May it be cursed for ever more,
The morning when I found that store!
When I found out my father is
A seedy little onanist.

For long after that shameful day
My heart was locked in gaol,
Burning with a fierce desire
To overthrow the male.
And lo! This band around my wrist
Has turned this dream to iron fist!

I find the thought repulses me
Of men behaving furtively
Their trousers down around their knees,
Where they think no one else can see,
Fat fingers clutching stubby shafts,
And tugging them till they go daft.

You wouldn't do it at the bus stop,
You wouldn't do it in a queue;
You wouldn't do it at the sweet shop,
Or with a large dog watching you;
You wouldn't for you know it's shameful –
You know that it's not very nice;
You wouldn't because it's disgraceful –
So heed you this, your Queen's advice!

On those who don't, my wrath shall fall
Swift, without mercy through the land!
For self-abusers one and all
Shall find their mucky pastimes banned!
My armies shall enforce my law,
Cleansing the filth that I abhor.

And while vile men tremble in fear
And give up what they once held dear,
Repenting of their wrong;
Her faithful servants far and near
Will watch for her to reappear
And know that Mother Feakle shan't be long!"

Then in a flash Queen Kitty's gone
Back to the place where she came from.

Part Five

Beaten subjects, the menfolk burn their passions

Our heroes cower lest they be seen
And hide within the shop;
Jack behind a salted horse
And Bill, up high, on top
Of a cabinet marked *Pixies Heads*,
They tremble there with fear and dread.

They watched in awe as formed a line,
The now transported thirty-nine
Proceed to the shop door;
 Each bearing that which he'd loved best
Over which to splash his mess
But never more.

Baldy King brought *Grannies' Bums*,
Jim Rix brought *Readers' Sisters*;
A maths teacher a book of sums,
"That's so disgusting, mister!"

Scrimp brought *Naughty Frills* and laughed
"Just topless, nothing sordid!"
But wedged inside he couldn't hide
His *Stiffs* (including *Morbid*).

Each tossed his object of desire
Into the empty, blameless street –
Then bowed and made a solemn vow
To keep his hands far from his meat.

Next, and rather sheepishly,
Came failed shoe salesman Tom:
He offered up the catalogue
That he'd kept hidden in his bog.

"I only got it for the slacks...
I needed a new pair...
But I never got beyond the page
Of women's underwear."

Tom the failed shoe salesman

Sir Scrotum Fromage De La Nobbe
Brought two young kittens, Bib and Bob;
Then local builder, Terry Spratt,
A pair of women's knickers that
He'd taken from the Smethursts' house
To fondle when he got aroused.

From the shop our heroes watched
These ominous proceedings;
"What can be going on?" asked Jack,
"And where do you think it's leading?"

Barley-Mow barged from the rear
"Out the way, you townie queers!
You don't have time for self-abuse
When you've got weasels on the loose
Spreading the clap to your dairy herd
By paddling in their new-laid turds!"

"Come, come, stout farmer," Smethurst breathed.
"Now what's that in your smock?"
Barley–Mow, he shook with tension –
"I thought it hardly worth the mention,
I get it monthly on subscription –
It's *Killing Hares by Electric Shock.*"

"Bring to me that sordid thing,
Corpulent son of soil!"
A voice boomed angry in the murk –
"Or, by Kit, I'll have your bowels!"

Farmer Barley-Mow

"*Gardadon! Gazeekel! Exubon! Feakle!*"
Words of ancient Cloudish, known to only but a few –
"*Zephalim! Huton! Zavaron! Luton!*"
Barley-Mow's old armpit glands had moved to somewhere new:
They dangled from beneath his throat,
Smearing his scarf of finest stoat.

The farmer fell to his stockinged knees,
And started pitifully sobbing:
"No animal will want me now,
Not even 'King Size' Dobbin!"

At length the pile stood ten foot high
And Smethurst raised his voice to cry:
"To Kitty, Queen, we sacrifice
To you these things that just aren't nice!"

Slowly, deliberately,
A dark-cloaked figure moved towards the pyre;
The other thirty-eight retired,
Murmuring:

"Bring the fire!
Bring the fire!
Let it cleanse our base desires!
Bring the fire!
Bring the fire!"
The voices gradually got higher.

"Cease!"
A long arm raised,
And lightning falls –
Igniting Giant Bill's old smalls –
And whoosh! – the bonfire too.

And in the light of that fierce blaze
Jack and Bill now see the face
Of he who life the bonfire gave
"By Wob!" cried Jack. "It's Wizard Dave!"

Part Six

*The spotty lad from Fogrunt bus station
wonders what the fates have in store*

In Bender's End across the Green,
Nearby the bridge that spans the stream,
Why! There's the nicest house you've seen:
The dwelling place of Widow Twinky
(A dear old crone, if somewhat stinky)
And a specky youth, aged seventeen.

A shy and nervous sort of boy,
His half-wit aunty's pride and joy,
He's happiest when left alone,
His nose stuck in a hefty tome –
Succumbs to frequent coughs and colds
And always does as he's been told –
Avoids the other boys' rough games,
Richard is the laddie's name.

In olden days, read Richard,
*Before the coming of the spoon,
Eating soup with nought but forks
Could take all afternoon.*
"Amazing!" gushed the pock-faced lad –
"Why do my friends say books are sad?"

Widow Twinky

"How was your day in Fogrunt Town?"
Aunt Betty asked once she'd sat down.
"And how's the job then? Still good fun?
Putting kippers into buns?"

The boy worked at a kipper stall
In Fogrunt, at the shopping mall.
His aunty's heart had glowed with pride
The day that he'd been notified
Of his successful interview –
"I always said, I always knew,
Where all your book learning'd get you!"

Now at the bottom of the lane
A small brown cow lived in a field.
He'd sometimes go and talk to her
Of wonders that his books revealed.

At other times he'd stand and tell
Of things that touched his heart as well.
He'd go there often, even lots,
And converse while he squeezed his spots.

Richard

"Dear Anabelle, my trusty friend!
I feel a weariness descend
When I reflect on what might be,
And on what shall become of me!"
He gave a little wistful sigh,
And squirted pus into his eye.

"I read in all my thrilling books
Of noble ventures undertook,
Of men who've done great, mighty deeds
Of heroes with their rampant steeds,
Of brave adventures out at sea –
And then I think, well, *look at me!*
Oh, Annabelle, there must be more!
There must be something I was born for!"

He gazed long at her swollen udders,
Gave a nervous smile, then shuddered.
"Me, I think I like them small,"
Then from nearby he heard a call.

"Well, that's it, my dear friend, goodbye!
I'm going for my tea!
I hear the voice of Aunty Betty,
She's made my favourite, tinned spaghetti!"

Part Seven

At Castle Flowery Dress, Kitty calls the tune

Smouldering in a scarlet gown,
Queen Kitty laughs in splendid scorn,
And eyes the wretch who's cast before
Her naked, abject, on the floor;
He'd been arrested late last night
And crapped his sequined pants in fright.

Now, smeared in his own excrement –
Dragged from his dungeon's foul confinement –
Stripped of all his sparkly raiment –
Summoned for Kit's entertainment –
She orders him "Before you swing
Upon the gibbet, you must sing!"

The crooner tries to stand but fails,
The palace guard strike him with flails;
At length, quite terrified, he wails:
"Please notice me!"

The queen then yawned and shook her head –
"It's strange, I used to think him great;
Now stretch his neck until he's dead,
And bring his goolies on a plate!"

Dwayne 'Jive Man' Malone

Poor Dwayne Malone just sobs and sobs,
Is dragged off by his private parts;
The Fogrunt Amulet throbs and throbs
And slowly hardens Kitty' heart.

Part Eight

*At Jack and Bill's cottage, the brown moth Blue
implores them to seek out Richard*

The dresser door stood open,
Jack was dusting down his muff –
"It's funny how she seems to gather
All these bits of fluff!"

Just then there came a tapping sound
Against the window pane:
Bill looked around but held his ground
"It's that brown moth again!"
While Jack just grinned but held his minge
"Perhaps she can explain!"

The moth divulged all that she'd seen
And all the places she had been;
She'd witnessed what had happened when
Kitty had shown a bit of chest,
And thus had turned all the king's men
Against their royal highness.

She'd seen all that had happened,
Wobblyknobble had been banished:
"I followed him down to the shops,
And then he simply vanished!
I only popped in for some scones,
But when I came out he was gone!"

Bill adjusted his cravat
Before a picture that
Bore the image of a whiskered gent
Wearing a cravat.

He moved along the off-white hall,
Stopped at the next pic on the wall,
(It was a maid brushing her hair),
Slicked back a curl and muttered "There!"

Blue whirled beneath the gas light
Like a conversational hand;
Impatient to explain to them
How dire, how grave,
How soon-enslaved
Was the future of Cloudland.

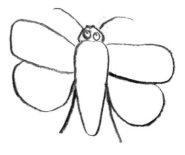

The Brown Moth Blue

"To what does the noble tree cling?
When the bitter wind does blow?
Its roots must cling firm to the ground,
For that is what they know."

"Where does the frightened tongue turn
When events prove it not brave?
It returns unto the safety
Of its own familiar cave."

"And now I turn to you, boys,
To help me with a quest!"
Bill stopped peering at a pic
Of a tramp scratching his vest.

"But it's too cold!" "We'll catch a chill!"
"I'm busy all next year!"
"It's Saturday!" "I'm feeling ill!"
But their cries Blue would not hear.

"First you must go to Bender's End
To find a young man who
Is crucial to fair Cloudland's fate
And everything you do.
For it's written by the ancient seers
That when the Queen of Dongs appears:

Lo! Let not fear's soft lichen creepe across thy breastbone.
Fie! For oe'r hunchback moor waits hinge-voiced boy,
Who cryeth not yet weepeth;
Weepeth from the sightless, dripping eyes upon his brow.
This is one to win the Dong Maid's heart
And bring her works to ruin!
And lo! Hie ye hence to where he clacks his bag of awkward bones,
To the East of Bumblybumble.

"I don't know who this laddie is,
I've no guess to his name;
But Bender's End's quite near to there,
You'd best leave soon, if it's all the same."

"Now, lads, I want you to beware,
For Kitty's spies are everywhere;
Your way is strewn with traps and snares,
Performing pigs and dancing bears;
Take heed, and trust not any soul,
No helpful elves nor friendly mole;
For things are other than they seem –
They may be servants of the queen!"

Blue led them out to a waiting cart
Laden with supplies:
"There's blankets, tents and muskets,
And ham and berry pies!"

Mustard, custard, parboiled bustard,
A grouse, a mouse, a pickled louse,
A chicken's leg, A parson's nose,
A vicar's ear, A verger's toes,
It stood before the house.

Blue waved a traceried wing goodbye,
And, with a little fluttering sigh,
Said "Good luck, giant and his mate!
You carry in your cart our fate!"

Part Nine

Cloudland's champions set out on their quest but are spied upon

The two both swore, they cursed, they grumbled,
As in their little cart they trundled;
"Why did she have to pick on us
To sort her fiddle-faddling fuss?"

Not half a mile from Cobblerswood,
Nearby the Stagnant Water,
They came upon a tinker man
Stood by a brightly-coloured van;
He waved hello, he waved good day,
They stopped to hear what he had to say,
Although they didn't oughter.

Arthur Slops

The pedlar introduced himself,
His name was Arthur Slops;
He showed them what he had to sell,
Some buckets and some mops –
"The widest range of household goods
And cheap at half the price!
Now, what'll you be having, gents?"
"Some tea towels would be nice."

They stopped and whiled a merry hour,
They told him all they had to tell –
About the recent goings on
And their visit from the moth as well.

"But not a word to anyone!"
Said Jack, about to leave.
"Your secret's safe," the pedlar winked,
And blew his nose upon his sleeve.

But all this while, perched high above,
Upon a nearby tree
A crow had heard their every word
And laughed mysteriously:
"So that's it, then! So that's their game!"
Black Derek was the foul bird's name.

Black Derek

Over the treetops Derek soared
With news for Kitty's ear;
No time to waste, he flew in haste,
With tidings she must hear.

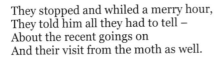

Part Ten

*Mr Flaps faces the truth of his sordid role in
the origins of Cloudland's peril*

With helpless panic, frightened squeaks,
Dad trembles underneath the sheets –
Each night, somewhere round three or four,
The shadows beckon at the door –
Poor Mr Flaps whines "Not again!"
The shadows laugh "Return! Return!" –
He's had the same nightmare for weeks.

Each night the dream threads the same path,
Into a dark black wood –
Darning the branches, gathering the trees,
Drawing them close like a dark black hood.

Each night the sleeper's dragged back to
That shameful forest scene –
The shadows make him look upon
A place that he'd once been –
That place he now regards with loathing
Where he'd removed his underclothing.

There she'd lain on a bed of leaves,
Slowly her sleeping body heaved –
"Now, don't be scared, I mean no harm,
Forgive my blind, presumptuous arm –
Forgive my fingers in their gloves,
They are the vanguard of my love –
I send them forth to gauge the land,
Swift on the horses of my hands."

"And what are these they ride across?
Studding your belly like stones in moss?
My word! But you're a saucy piece
With your turned-up nose and forty teats!"

"You know you want it, don't you, dear?
For see! You're getting moist!"
There's no one else around to hear –
His britches he unhoists.
There, amongst tangled thorns and twigs,
He'd known the forty-teated pig.

Flaps awoke and found he lay
Aside the blanket box –
Fingers working madly
At the hinges and the locks.

"Oh, why did I? Oh, how did I?
Oh, what have I become?"
Condemned to recall what he did,
He knew not what he'd done.

Part Eleven

Still condemned to the wilderness, Wobblyknobble is wild with grief

The denizens of this grim place
Have nineteen words for 'grey';
Including *gresh* and *slunt* and *sluff*
And *gusset-underlay.*

But twenty shades of sombre
Had settled on the soul
Of good King Wobblyknobble
Who's been banished to the cold.

Banished to this lowland mire,
Though he'd done nothing wrong –
Alone but for a donkey
And a barber with some tongs

Delirious with hunger,
Wob spied a cut of beef –
He looked again and found it was
A child's soiled handkerchief.

He thought he saw a roasted quail
Revolving on a spit –
He looked again and saw it was
An old dry-cleaning chit.

He raised his head and in a voice
That care had rendered harsh,
He cried across the drabness
Like a bittern in the marsh.
Like a bittern in the marsh.

Here Ends Book Four

The Great Black Sow

Index

IRON Press is among the country's longest
established independent literary publishers.
The press began operations in 1973 with IRON
Magazine which ran for 83 editions until 1997.
Since 1975 we have also brought out a regular
list of individual collections of poetry, fiction and
drama plus various anthologies ranging from *Voices
of Conscience, Limerick Nation, The Poetry of
Perestroika, 100 Island Poems* and *Cold Iron, Ghost
Stories from the 21st Century.*

The press is one of the leading independent
publishers of haiku in the UK.
Since 2013 we have also run a regular IRON Press
Festival round the harbour in our native Cullercoats.
IRON in the Soul, our third festival,
was staged in Summer 2017; a fourth festival,
IRON OR takes place in June 2019.

We are delighted to be a part of
Inpress Ltd, which was set up by Arts Council
England to support independent literary publishers.
Go to our website (www.ironpress.co.uk)
for full details of our titles and activities.